From Concept to Creation
MAKING ENTERTAINMENT

ROAR!

# HOW Comics and Manga ARE MADE

by Noah Leatherland

BEARPORT PUBLISHING

Minneapolis, Minnesota

**Credits**

Images are courtesy of Shutterstock.com, unless otherwise stated. COVER & RECURRING – Tutatamafilm, Udurrvf3Rd, inithings, Anastasia Boiko, Dooder, Rolau Elena, yopinco, Mironov Konstantin. 4–5 – Krakenimages.com, Ryan DeBerardinisa. 8–9 – Jamess_W, M. Faisal Riza. 10–11 – Prostock-studio, wavebreakmedia. 12–13 – Frame Stock Footage, Sensay. 14–15 – Ground Picture, megaflopp. 16–17 – Chaosamran_Studio, Dyto Yudistiro. 18–19 – Chaiwuth Wichitdho, David Lichtneker/Alamy Stock Photo. 20–21 – Tan Tantra Maulana, Tutatamafilm. 22–23 – MarbellaStudio. 24–25 – HerArtSheLoves, BongkarnGraphic. 28–29 – Frank Parker, Lewis Tse. 30–31 – Prostock-studio.

**Bearport Publishing Company Product Development Team**

Publisher: Jen Jenson; Director of Product Development: Spencer Brinker; Editorial Director: Allison Juda; Editor: Cole Nelson; Editor: Tiana Tran; Production Editor: Naomi Reich; Art Director: Kim Jones; Designer: Kayla Eggert; Designer: Steve Scheluchin; Production Specialist: Owen Hamlin

Library of Congress Cataloging-in-Publication Data is available at www.loc.gov or upon request from the publisher.

ISBN: 979-8-89577-084-9 (hardcover)
ISBN: 979-8-89577-474-8 (paperback)
ISBN: 979-8-89577-201-0 (ebook)

© 2026 BookLife Publishing
This edition is published by arrangement with BookLife Publishing.

North American adaptations © 2026 Bearport Publishing Company. All rights reserved. No part of this publication may be reproduced in whole or in part, stored in any retrieval system, or transmitted in any form or by any means, electronic, mechanical, photocopying, recording, or otherwise, without written permission from the publisher. Bearport Publishing is a division of FlutterBee Education Group.

For more information, write to Bearport Publishing, 3500 American Blvd W, Suite 150, Bloomington, MN 55431.

# Contents

How Things Are Made . . . . . . . . . . . . . . 4
On the Page . . . . . . . . . . . . . . . . . . . . . . 6
Comics vs. Manga . . . . . . . . . . . . . . . . . 8
Ideas and Imagination . . . . . . . . . . . . . 10
Story and Characters . . . . . . . . . . . . . 12
Script Writing . . . . . . . . . . . . . . . . . . . . 14
Character Design . . . . . . . . . . . . . . . . . 16
Storyboards . . . . . . . . . . . . . . . . . . . . . 18
Penciling . . . . . . . . . . . . . . . . . . . . . . . . 20
Inking and Coloring . . . . . . . . . . . . . . . 22
Lettering . . . . . . . . . . . . . . . . . . . . . . . . 24
Covers. . . . . . . . . . . . . . . . . . . . . . . . . . 26
Release . . . . . . . . . . . . . . . . . . . . . . . . 28
Your Next Project . . . . . . . . . . . . . . . . . 30
Glossary . . . . . . . . . . . . . . . . . . . . . . . . 31
Index . . . . . . . . . . . . . . . . . . . . . . . . . . 32
Read More . . . . . . . . . . . . . . . . . . . . . . 32
Learn More Online . . . . . . . . . . . . . . . . 32

# How Things Are Made

Are you a creative person?

Your favorite comic books, movies, TV shows, and video games came from the minds of people just like you!

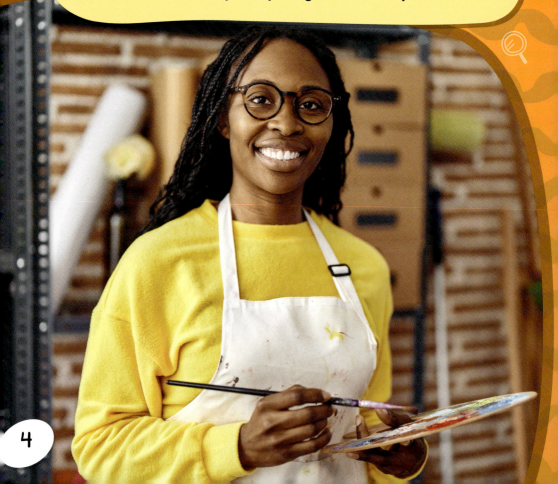

Comics and manga are stories told with pictures as well as words. They are often sold as books.

There are many steps to making these forms of entertainment. It takes a group of talented people to turn a concept into a bestselling comic or manga.

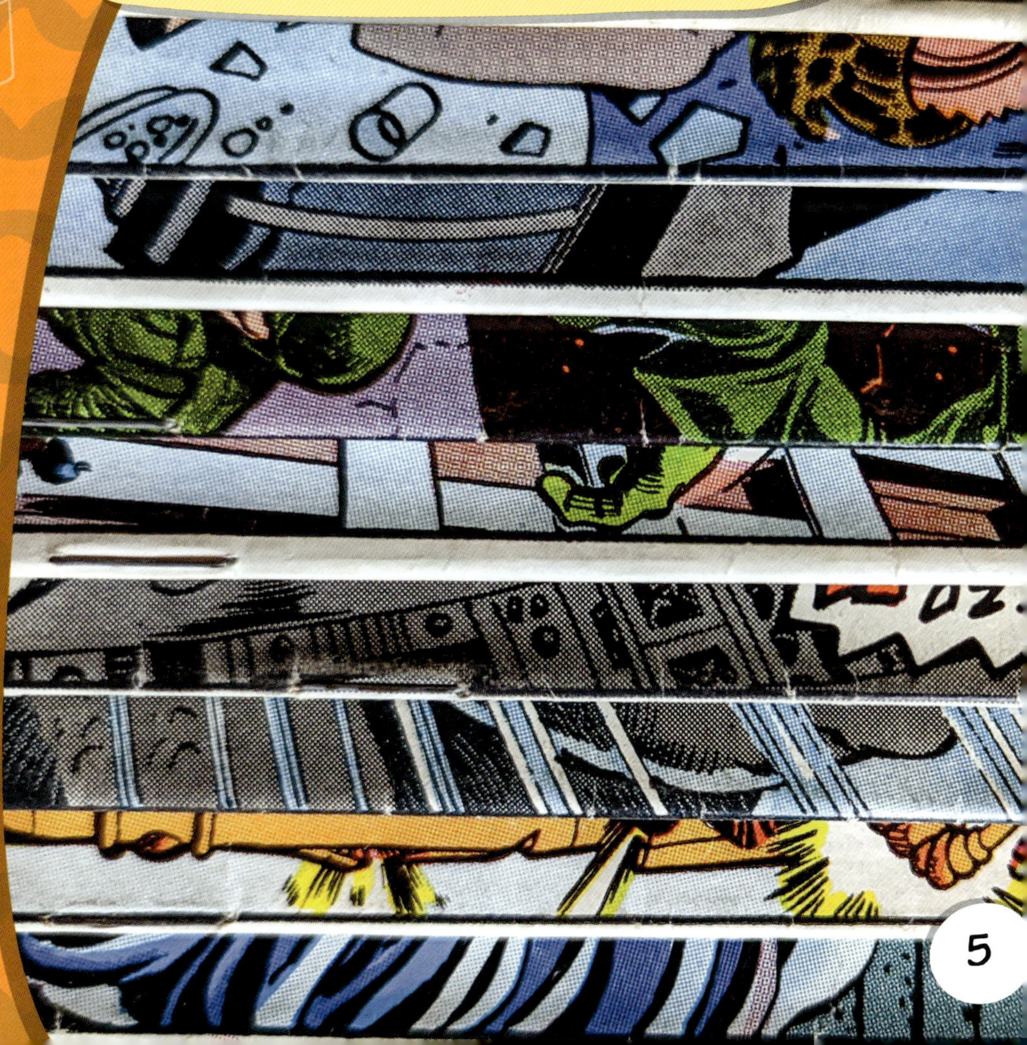

# On the Page

Comics and manga tell stories in a visual way. Both have pages broken up into panels, or frames. These panels each have a drawing that tells part of the story.

Some pages have lots of panels. Other pages might have one big panel.

There is often also text. Words that characters say are written in speech bubbles.

Some panels have captions that help tell the story.

Sometimes, words are added to describe sounds.

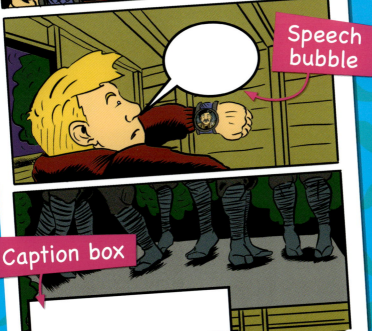

Speech bubble

Caption box

# Comics vs. Manga

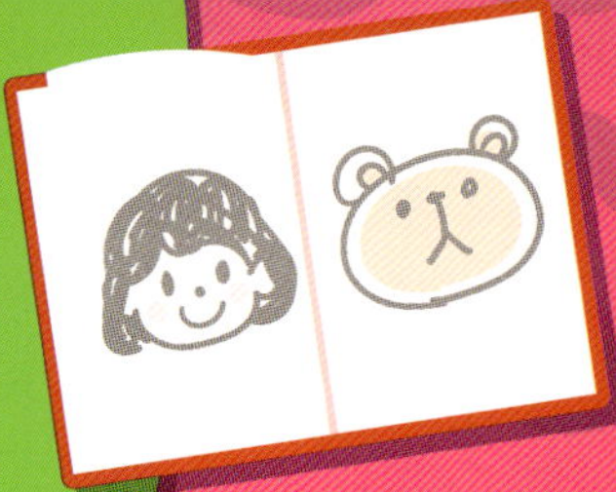

Comics and manga look very similar. However, there are some key things that make them different.

Manga are usually black and white. Comics often have color.

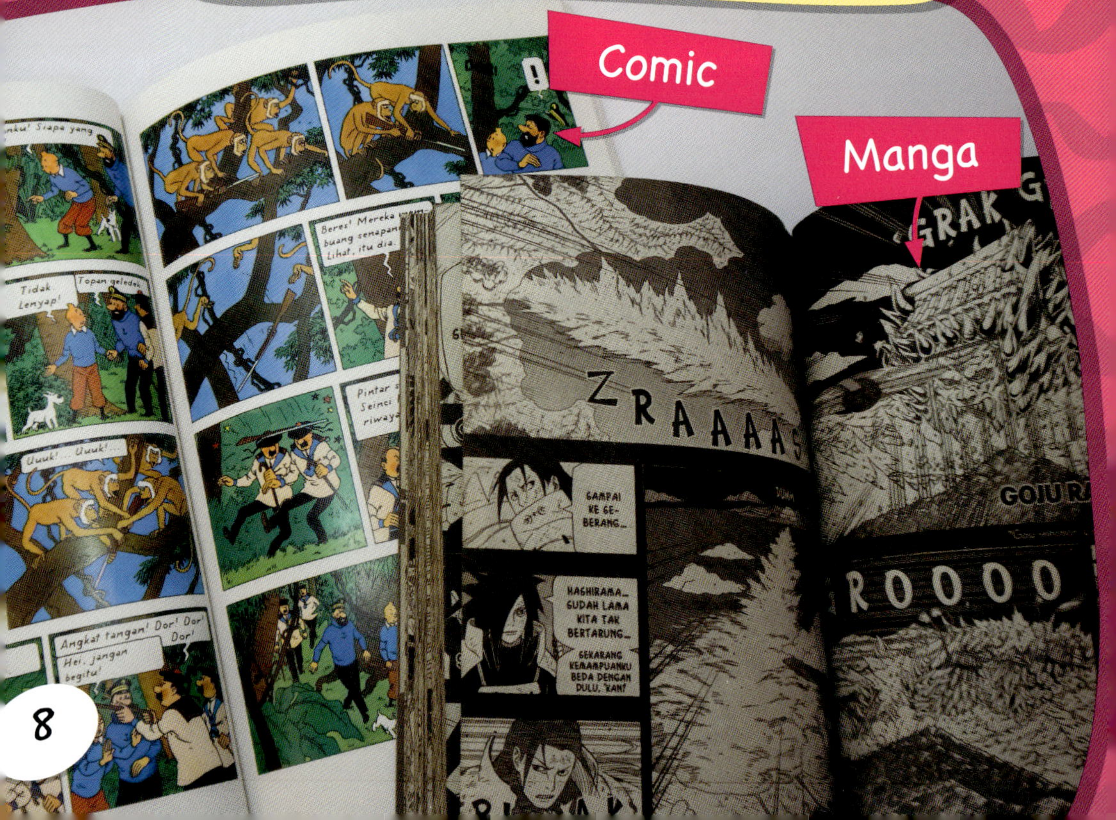
Comic
Manga

Also, comics are read from left to right. Manga are often read from right to left.

This is because manga stories come from Japan, where books are read from right to left. But comics come from all over the world.

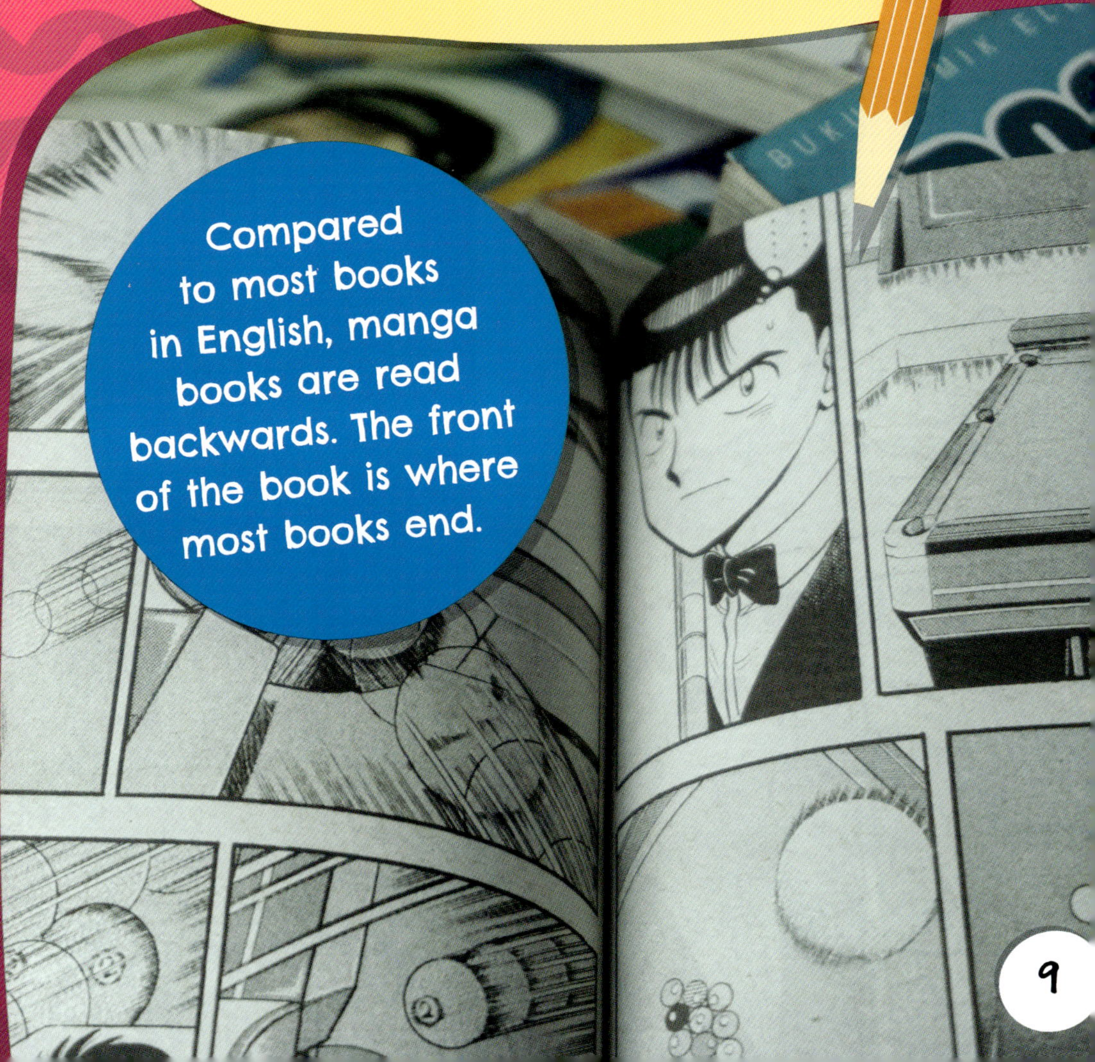

Compared to most books in English, manga books are read backwards. The front of the book is where most books end.

# Ideas and Imagination

The first step in creating a comic or manga is to have an idea.

No idea is too big. Comics and manga can tell all kinds of stories. They can be scary, funny, exciting, relaxing, or anything else you want.

Artists, writers, and **editors** often work together to think of ideas. However, manga usually have the same person drawing and writing. This person is called a **mangaka** (MAHN-gah-kah).

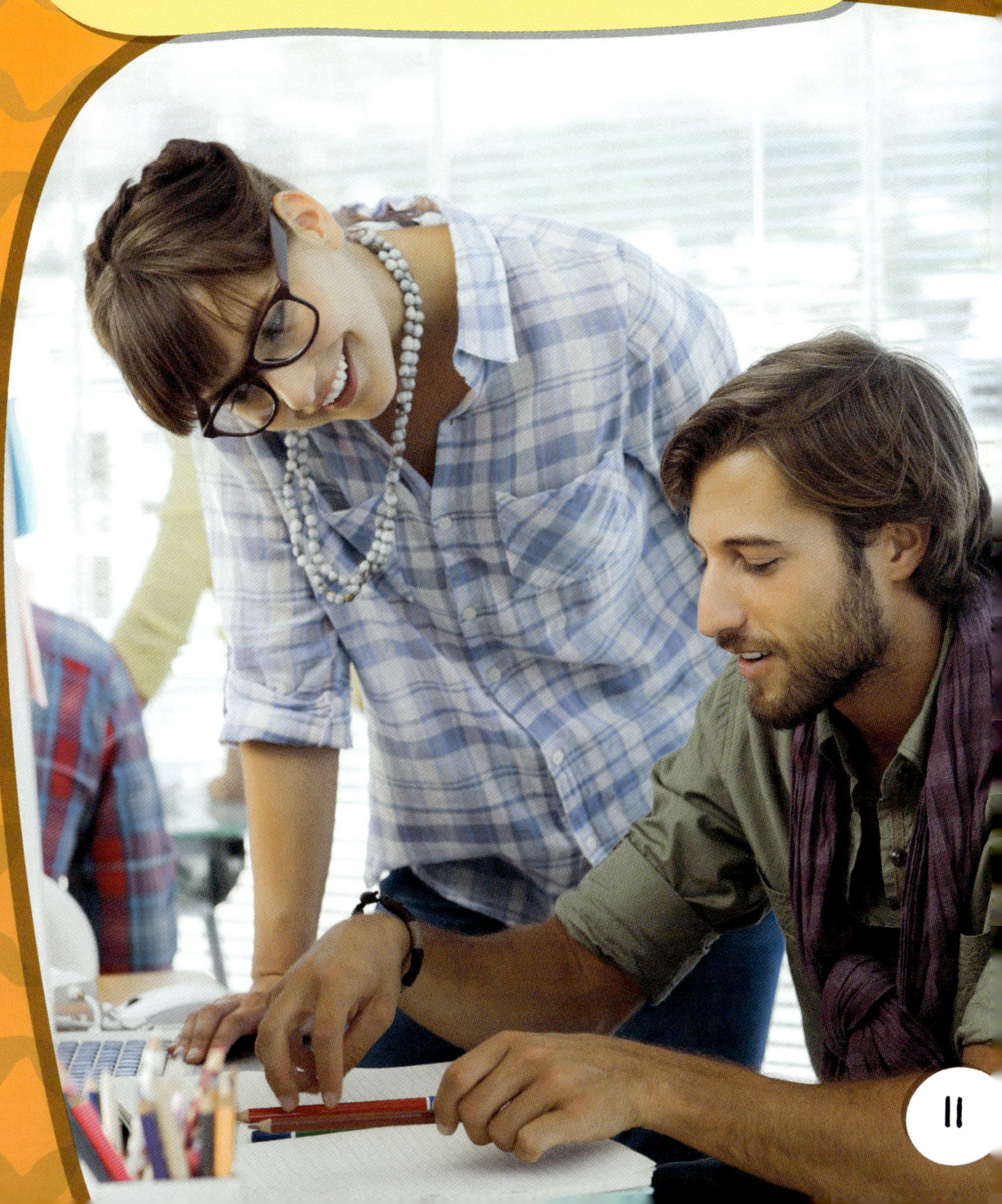

# Story and Characters

After deciding on an idea, the writer or artist needs to create a story. This story should have a beginning, middle, and end.

Almost all stories have characters. Often, the characters don't stay the same. They change by the end of a story.

Sometimes, characters in comics and manga are powerful heroes. But not always. Some of the most famous characters in these stories are normal, everyday people.

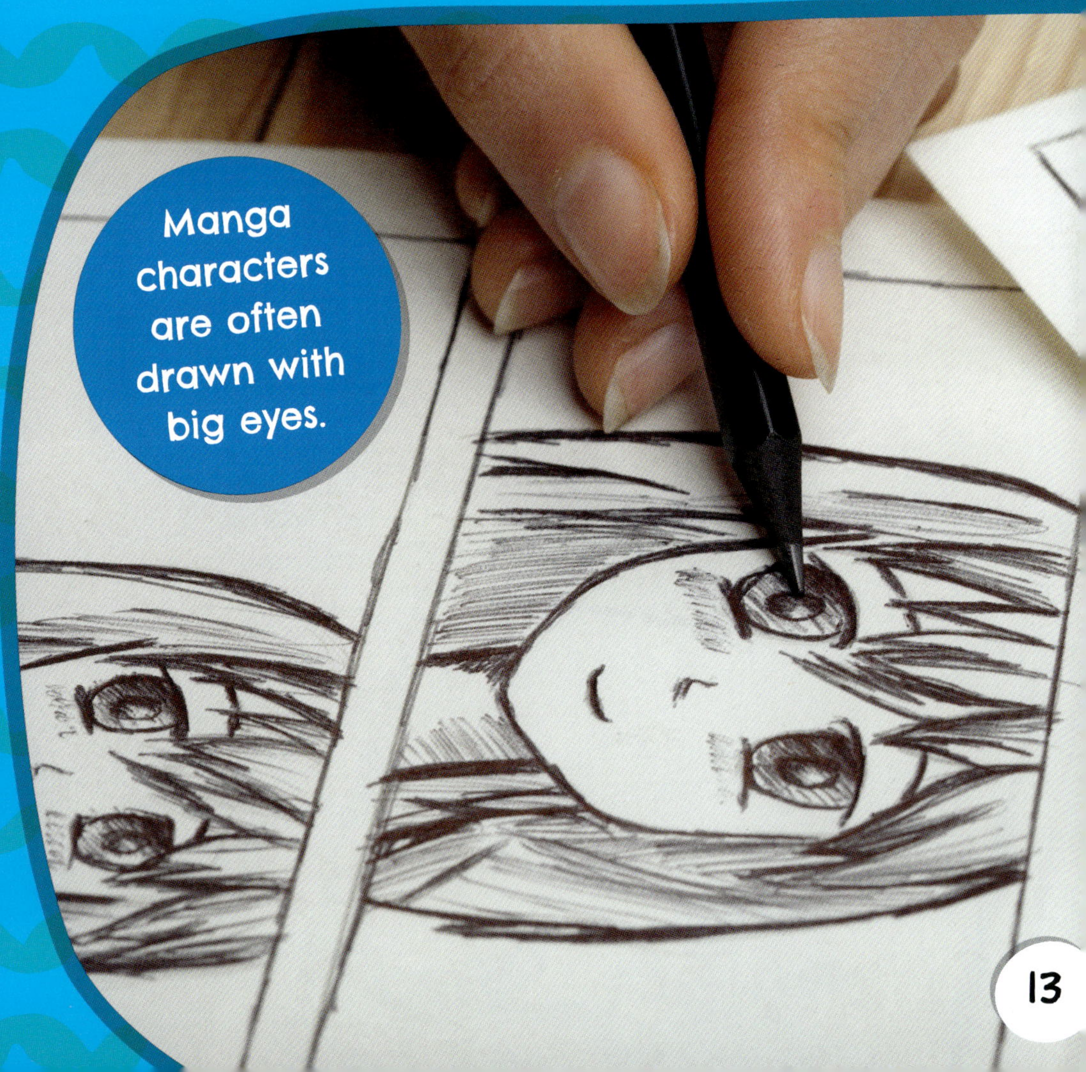

Manga characters are often drawn with big eyes.

# Script Writing

The next step is to turn the story into a script. This tells an artist what goes on each page. The script also describes the **setting**.

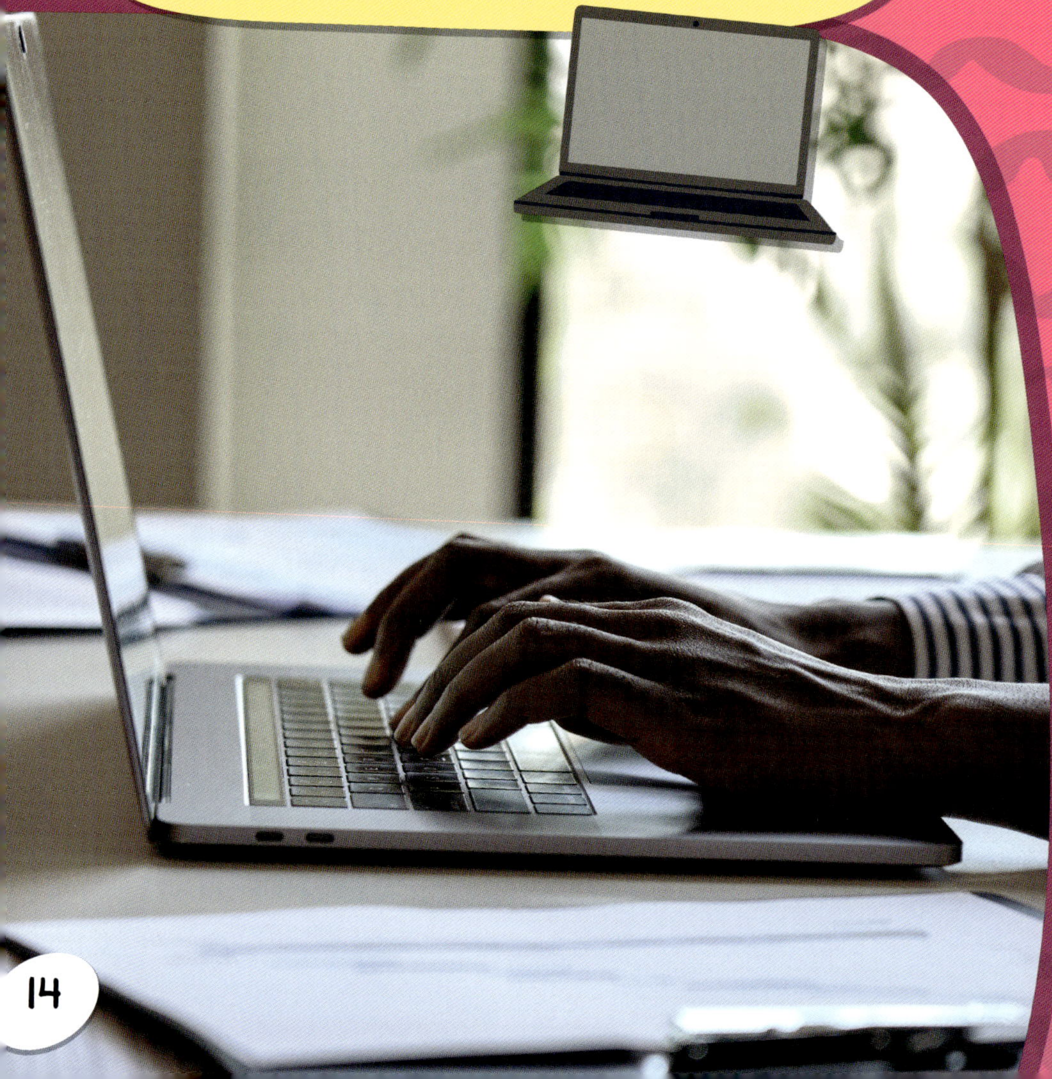

Some scripts have lots of detail. Others let the artists have more freedom to decide what to draw.

It is important that the writer and the artist work together to turn the script into a great book.

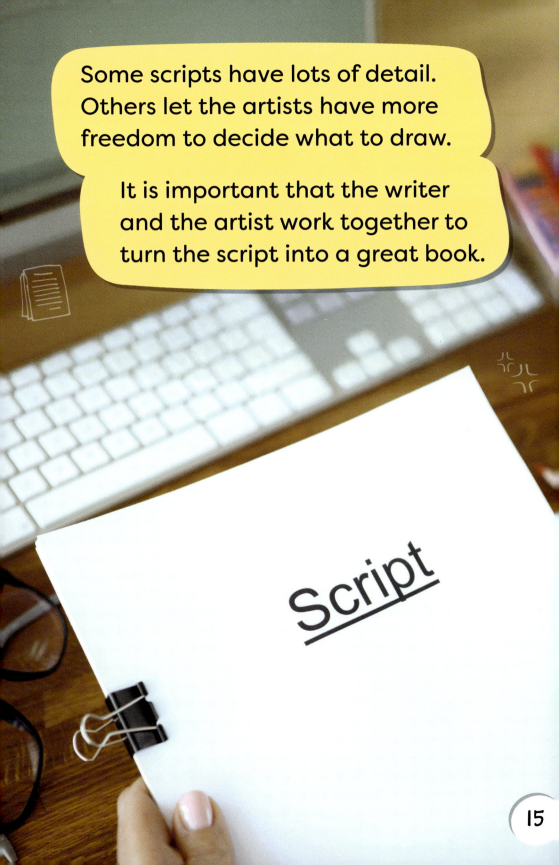

# Character Design

Once the script is written, a comic or manga artist needs to **design** the characters.

Some characters might have been sketched in the early planning stage. But now it is time to decide on a final look.

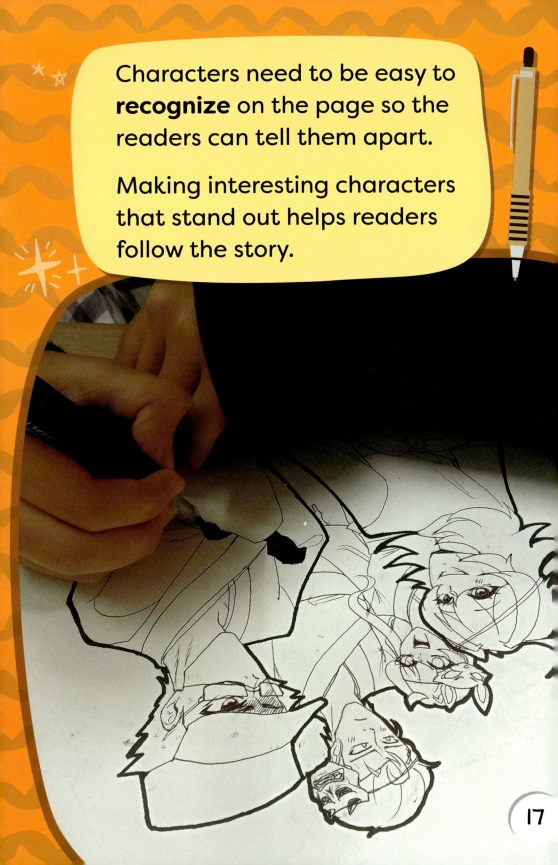

Characters need to be easy to **recognize** on the page so the readers can tell them apart.

Making interesting characters that stand out helps readers follow the story.

# Storyboards

Before they draw the story, comic artists and mangaka make a rough sketch of each page.

Comic artists draw where the panels will go and sketch what will be shown in each one. This is called a thumbnail.

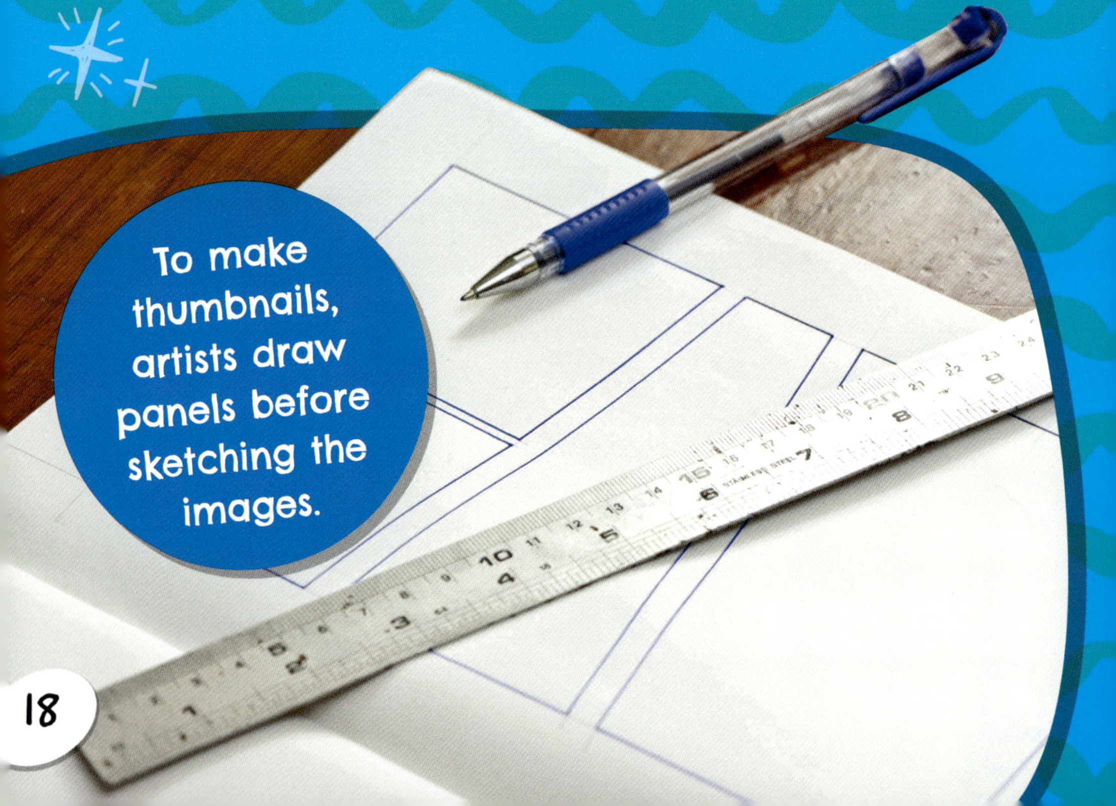

To make thumbnails, artists draw panels before sketching the images.

Mangaka do something similar. They sketch the pages and include the characters' **dialogue** in speech bubbles.

This kind of sketch is called a name. Editors review the name to make sure it looks good before the mangaka draws the final art.

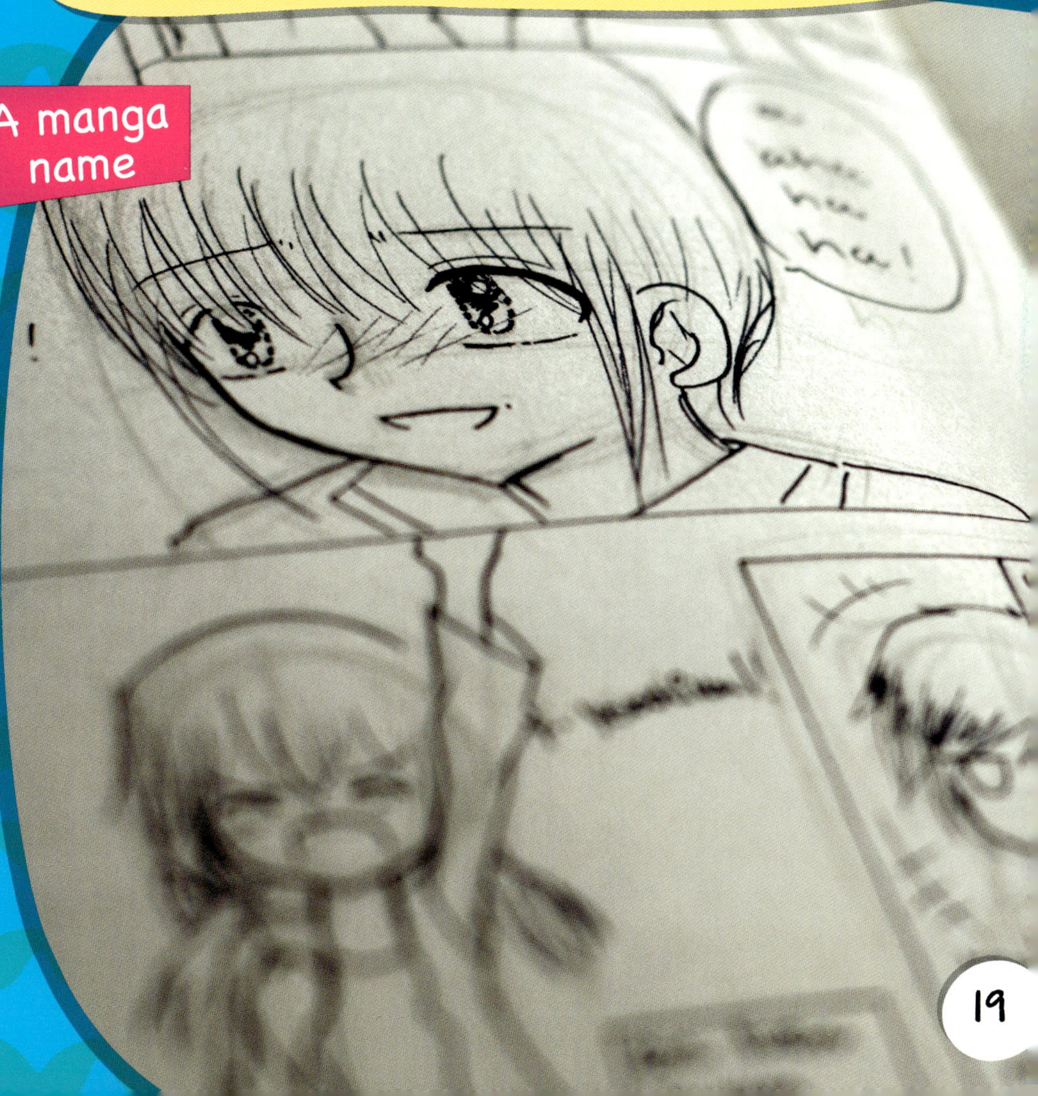

A manga name

# Penciling

Now, work on the final art can begin. In comics, this next step is called penciling.

This art used to be drawn on paper using pencils. Many comics are now drawn **digitally**.

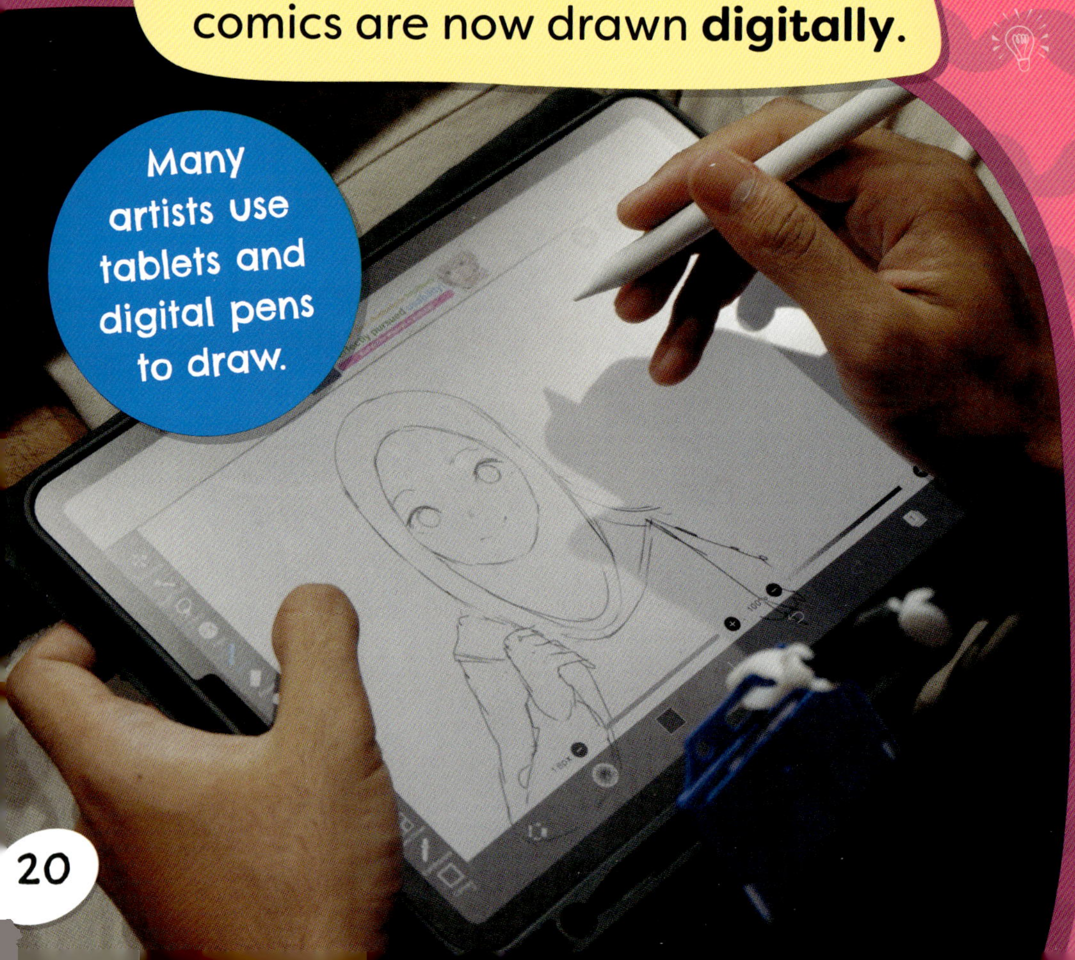

Many artists use tablets and digital pens to draw.

Digital art is much easier to fix. Tapping a screen takes less time and effort than using an eraser!

Writers and editors check the penciling work. They make sure everything looks right before moving to the next steps.

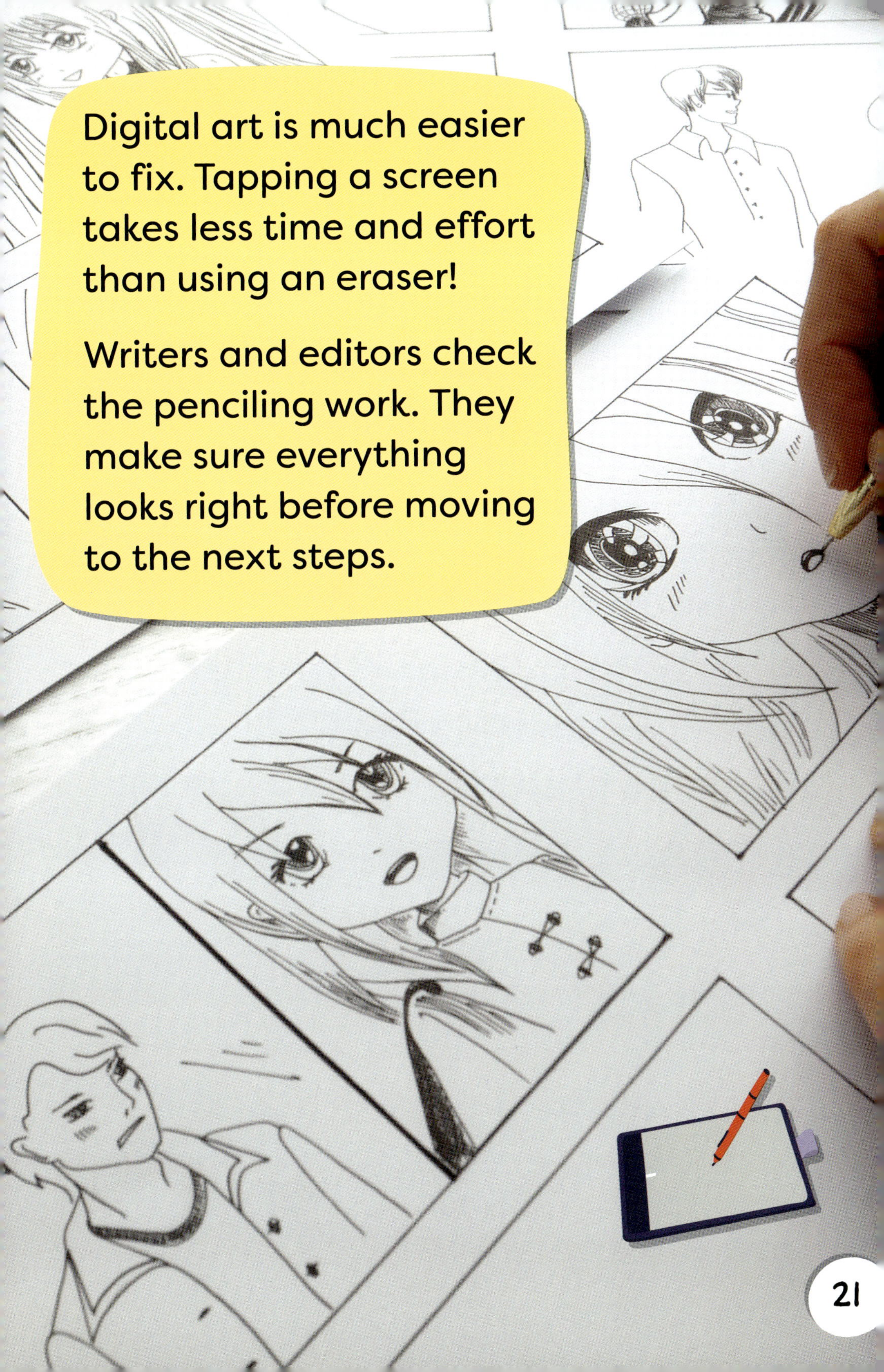

# Inking and Coloring

Inking comes after penciling. This is where the black lines and dark areas are filled in. It is called inking because comic artists used to use ink pens to fill in the pencil lines. Some artists still do!

For manga that are black and white, the art is finished after this step.

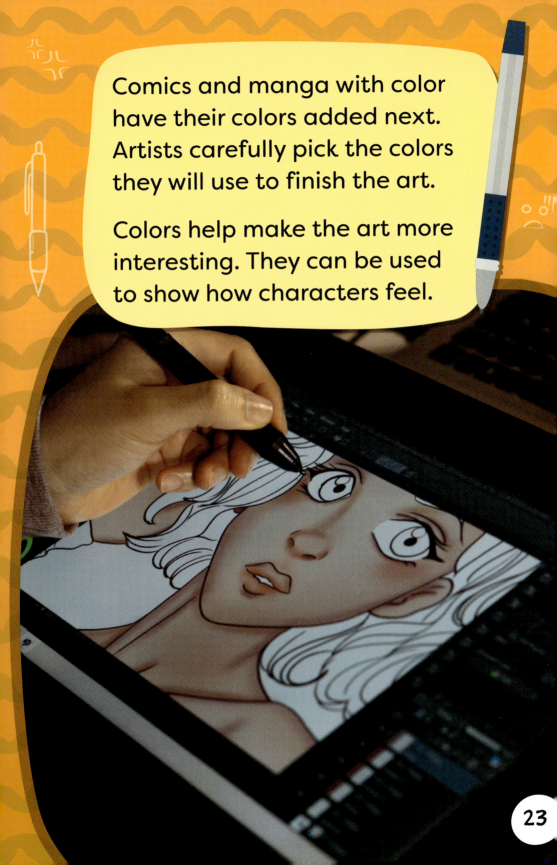

Comics and manga with color have their colors added next. Artists carefully pick the colors they will use to finish the art.

Colors help make the art more interesting. They can be used to show how characters feel.

# Lettering

Lettering is the stage where words are added to the panels. Letterers add speech bubbles, captions, and sound effects to panels to tell the story.

Different styles of letters can add more feelings to the words.

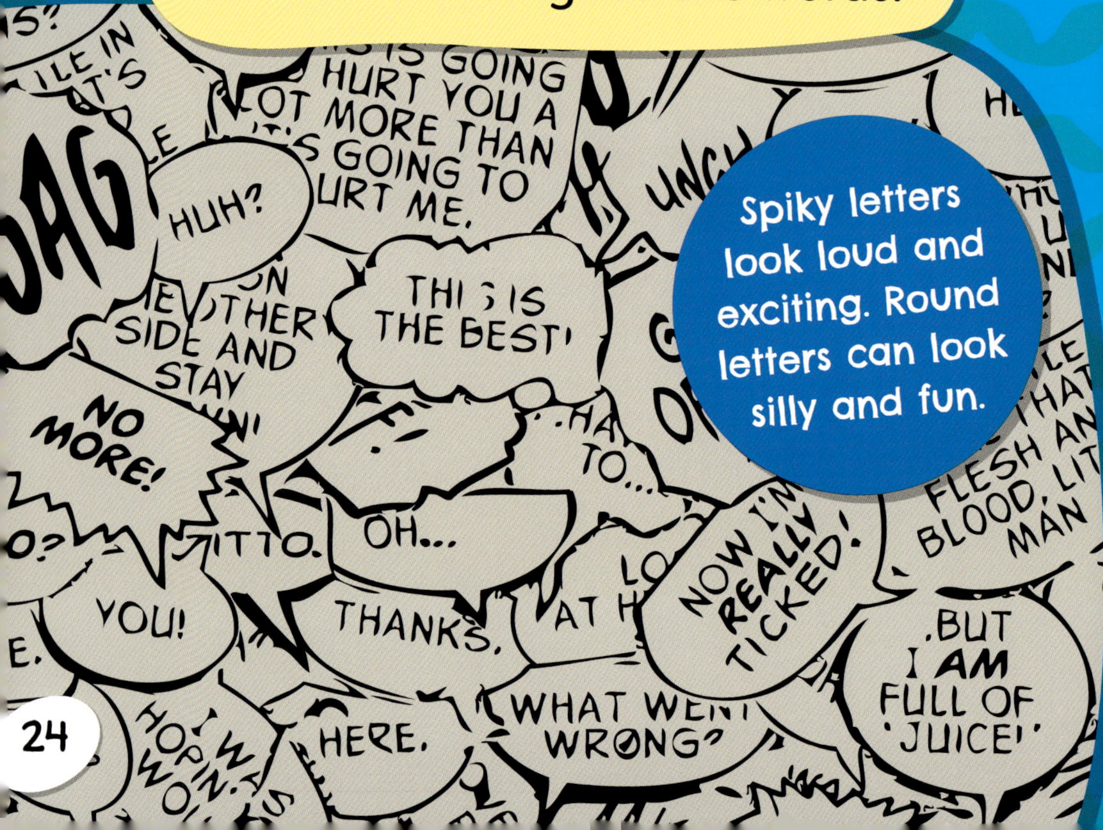

HUH?
NO MORE!
OH...
YOU!
THANKS.
HERE.
WHAT WENT WRONG?
NOW I'M REALLY TICKED!
.BUT I AM FULL OF JUICE!


Spiky letters look loud and exciting. Round letters can look silly and fun.

If the mangaka added text to the name sketch, that text is now added to the final art in a clearer **font**.

The book is almost complete. All that is left to make is the cover.

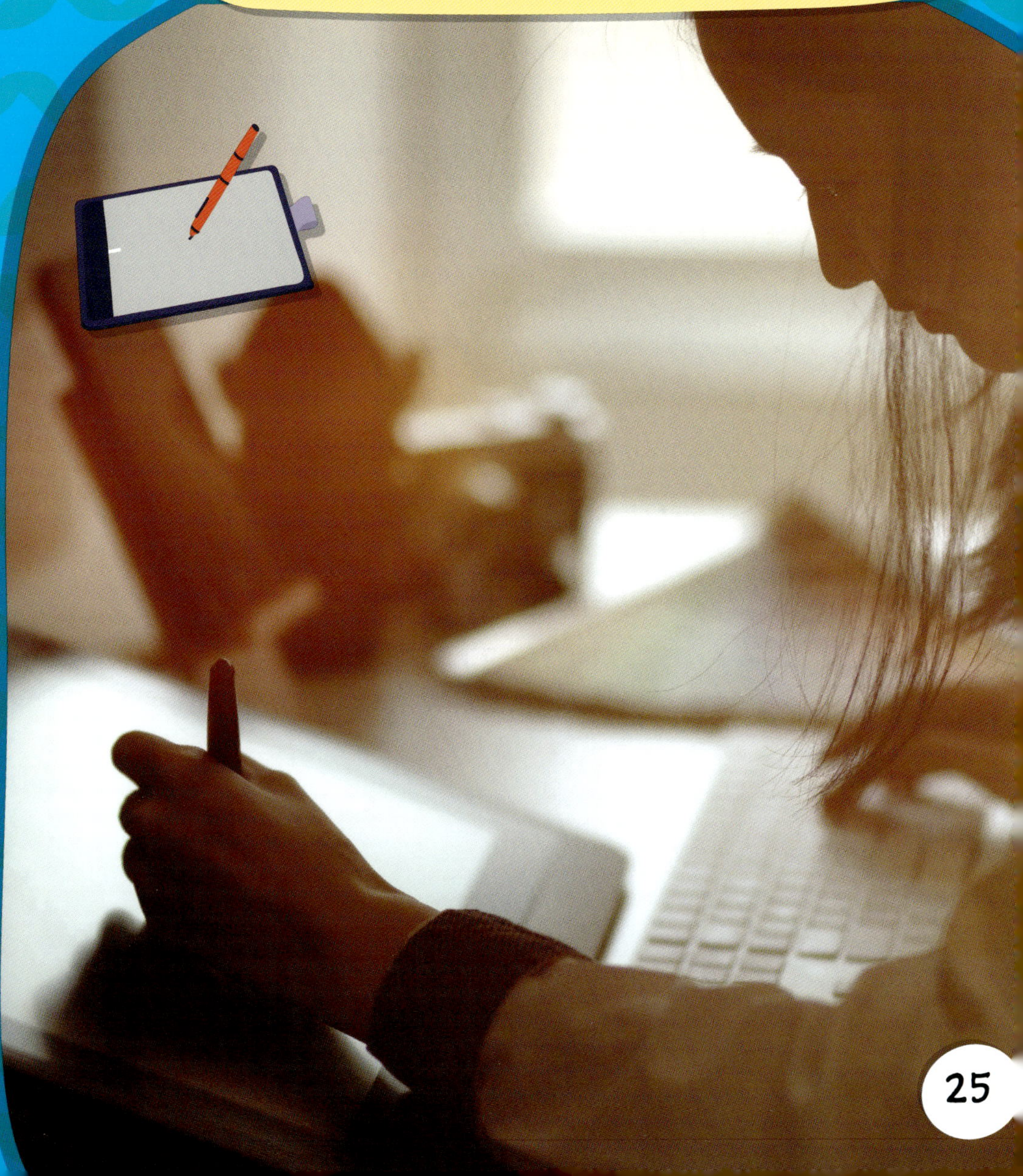

# Covers

Covers are usually the first thing people see when they look at comic books or manga.

An eye-catching cover will **encourage** people to pick up and read the book.

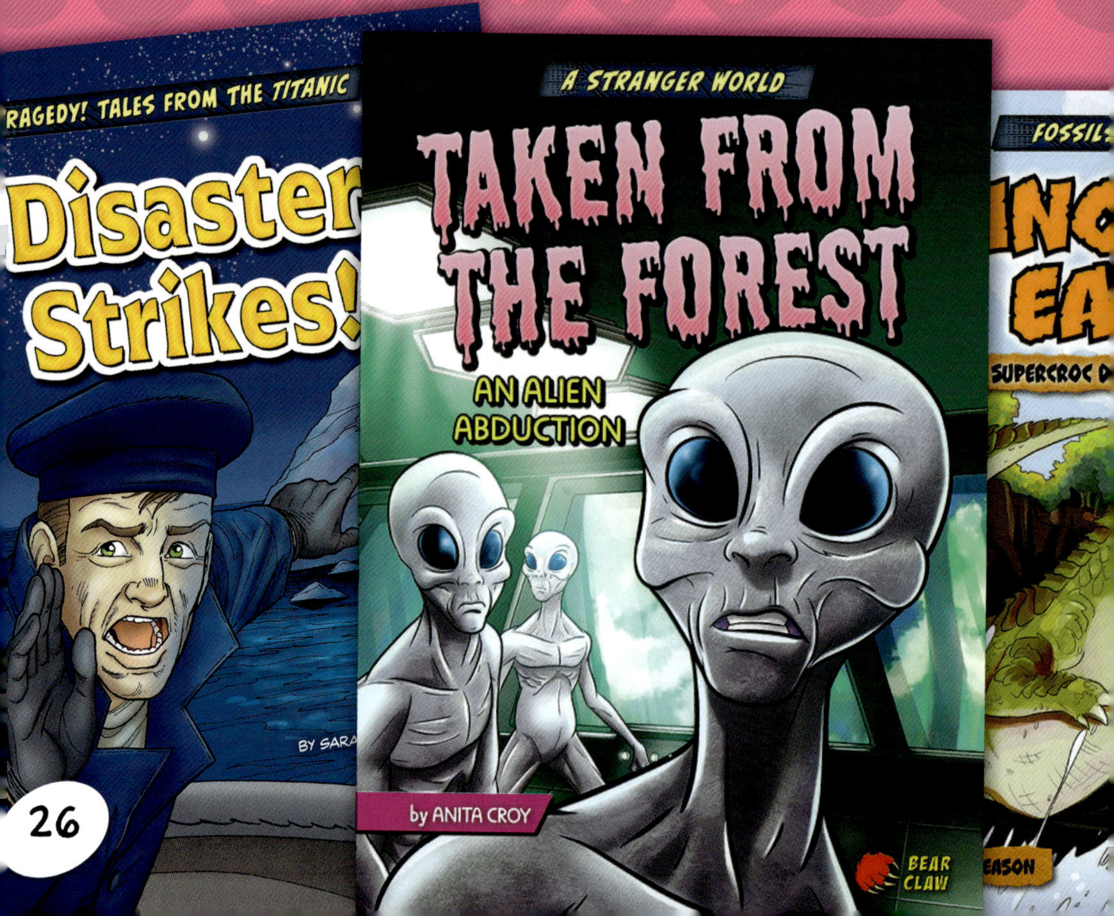
RAGEDY! TALES FROM THE TITANIC
Disaster Strikes!
BY SARA
A STRANGER WORLD
TAKEN FROM THE FOREST
AN ALIEN ABDUCTION
by ANITA CROY
BEAR CLAW
FOSSIL
SUPERCROC

Covers usually give the reader an idea of what the book is about. Artists spend a lot of time designing covers.

Sometimes, a comic book has a few different covers. This encourages people to buy more and collect every cover!

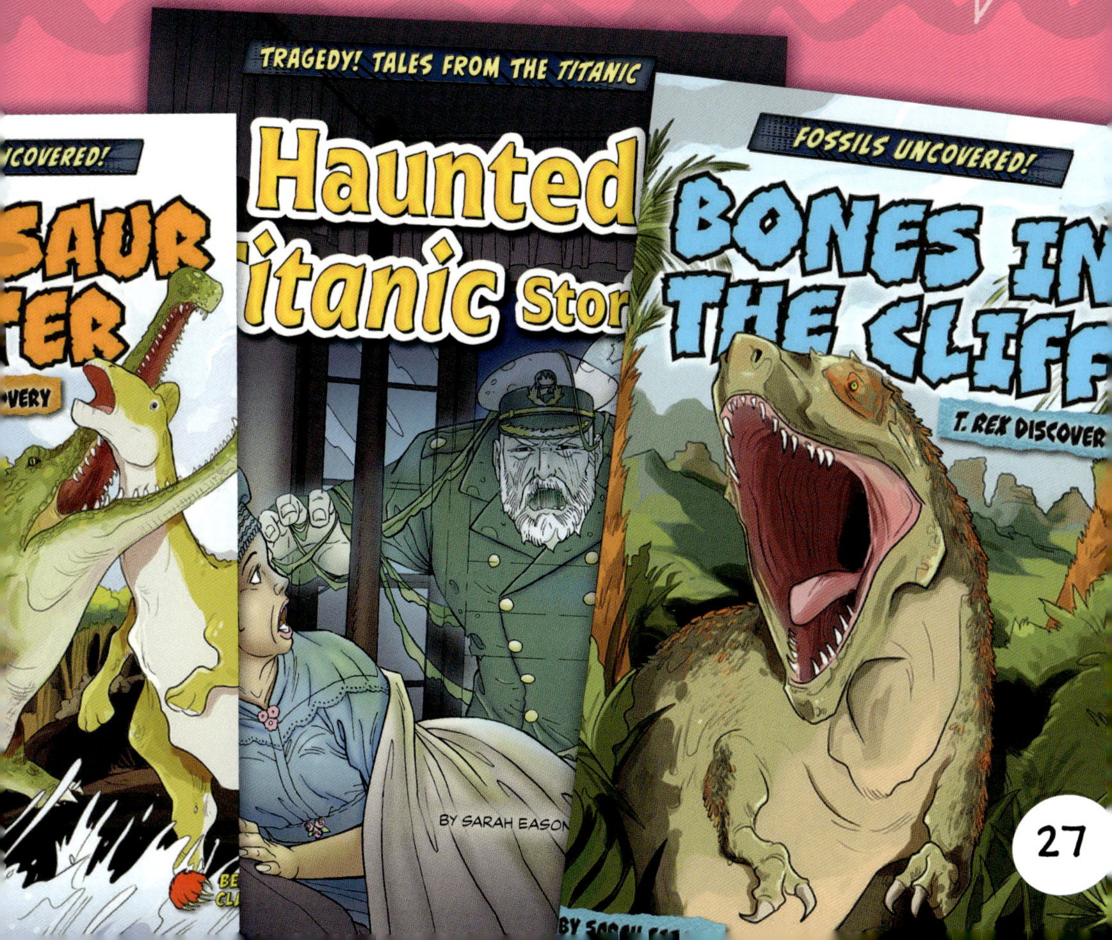
TRAGEDY! TALES FROM THE TITANIC
Haunted
itanic Stor
BY SARAH EASON
FOSSILS UNCOVERED!
BONES IN
THE CLIFF
T. REX DISCOVER

# Release

Some comics and manga are printed to be sold in shops. Others are found only online.

Often, comic stories are released in parts called issues. Some issues are printed in magazines. Others are collected into books called graphic novels.

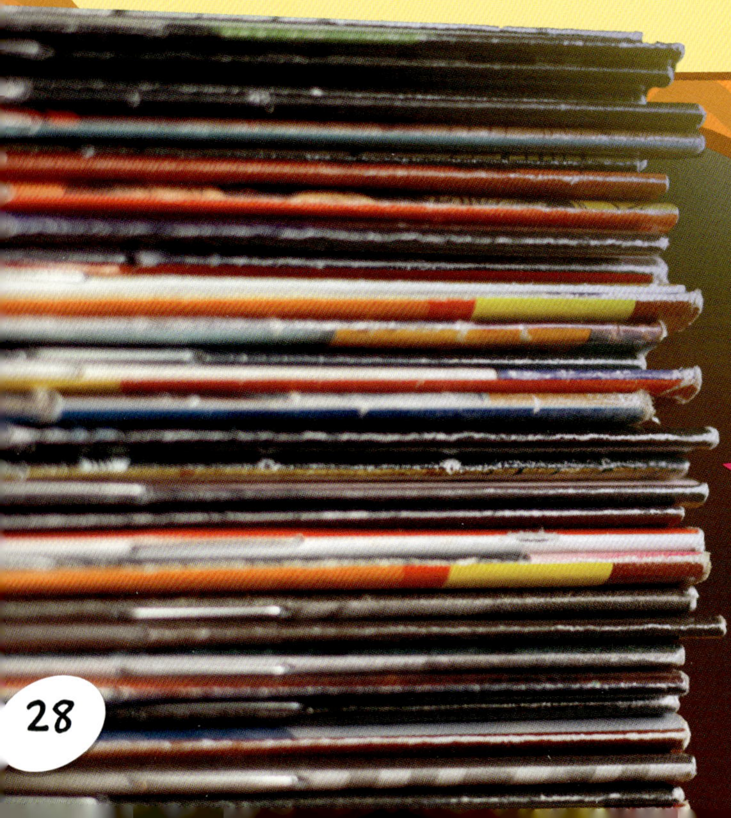

Comic issues

Lots of manga stories are released as part of a magazine. A manga magazine usually has several stories from different mangaka.

If a manga is very popular, it might get released as its own book.

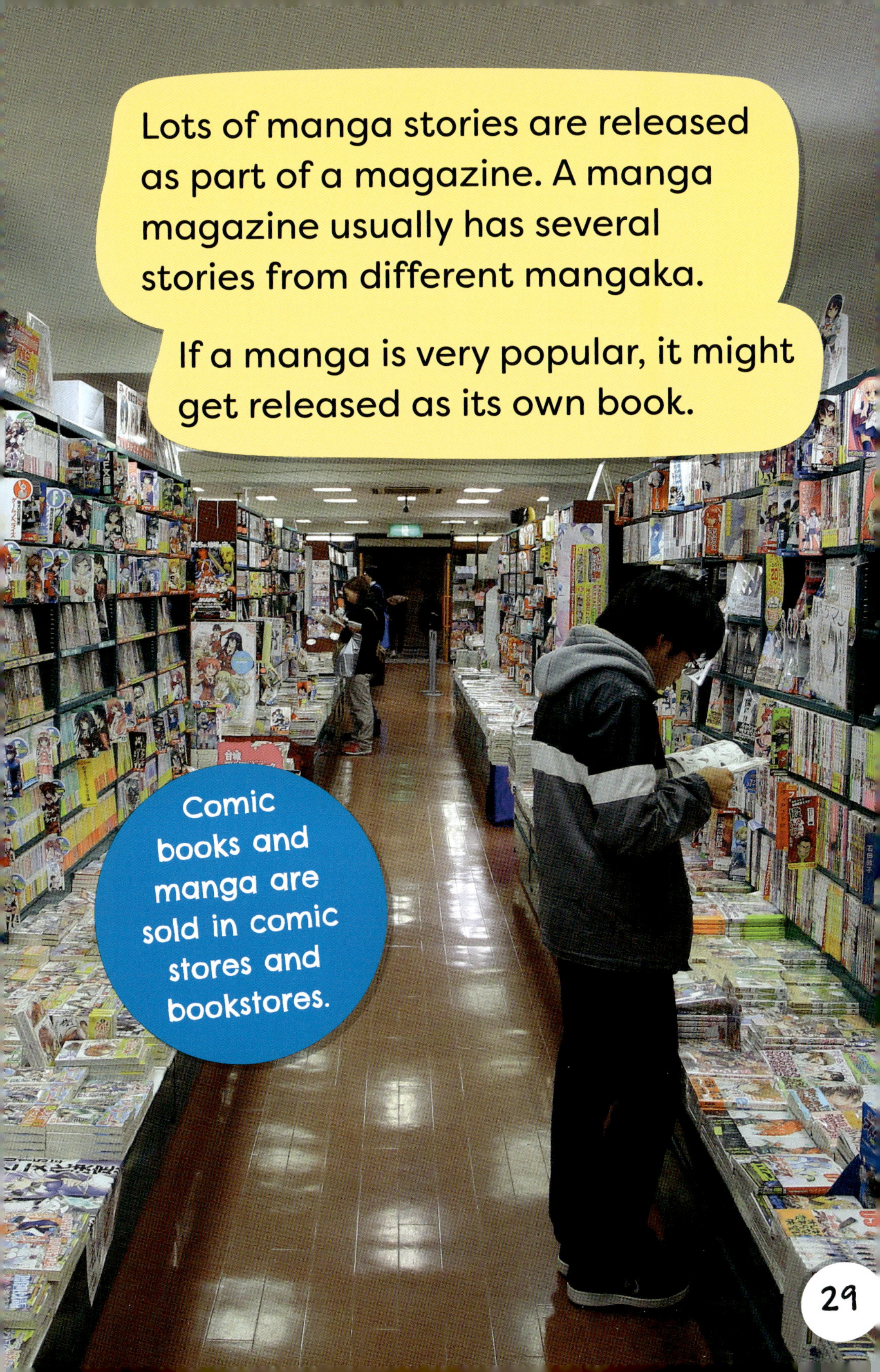

Comic books and manga are sold in comic stores and bookstores.

# Your Next Project

Creating comics and manga takes hard work. But that work can be a lot of fun!

Do you want to make your own comic or manga? What would you do to create one? The next bestseller could be yours!

# Glossary

**design** the way something looks

**dialogue** words spoken between two or more characters

**digitally** related to computers or other electronic devices

**editors** people who check someone's work and suggest ways to make it better

**encourage** to make a person want to do something

**font** the design of letters on a page

**mangaka** a professional manga writer and artist

**recognize** to spot something that is already known

**setting** the location in which a story takes place

# Index

**editors** 11, 19, 21
**graphic novels** 28
**heroes** 13
**issues** 28
**magazines** 28–29
**mangaka** 11, 18–19, 25, 29
**panels** 6–7, 18, 24
**paper** 20
**writers** 11–12, 15, 21

# Read More

**Harris, Scott.** *Manga Heroes (Draw Manga Style).* Beverly, MA: Quarry, 2023.

**Leatherland, Noah.** *How Anime and Cartoons Are Made (From Concept to Creation).* Minneapolis: Bearport Publishing Company, 2026.

# Learn More Online

1. Go to **FactSurfer.com** or scan the QR code below.
2. Enter "**Comics and Manga**" into the search box.
3. Click on the cover of this book to see a list of websites.